Contents

Beginning Sequencing

Sequence Events

Use familiar activities and items to dramatize real-life events in the correct sequence. Begin by showing an item or group of items and explain what you are about to do ("I'm going to put on my sweater."). Then begin putting on the sweater incorrectly (button the sweater and attempt to put it on). Stop when children say you are doing it wrong. Have someone come up and show the correct way to put it on.

Follow the same procedure with other common activities:
- putting on shoes and socks (sock first, tie laces, then try to put shoe on foot)
- washing hands (put soap on hands, dry on towel, then put hands in water)
- setting the table for lunch (put plates on table, cover with tablecloth or place mat, put food on cloth instead of plate.)

When children are successful at sequencing an activity using real objects, ask them to give oral directions telling how something is done.

Sequence Items in a Series

Introduce vocabulary used to describe an item's position in a series (first, second, third, etc.; before, after that, last) as you do the following activity with children.

Teacher puts three objects in a row, points to each object, and tells where it is ("The apple is first, the banana is in the middle, the orange is last.") The items are then given to three children who are asked to put them in the correct order.

As children have more experience sequencing items, introduce the terms second, third, fourth, and fifth. Then repeat the activity with four or five items.

 Sequencing • EMC 737

Sequence Nursery Rhymes

Use familiar nursery rhymes such as Little Miss Muffet to practice sequencing pictures.

Preparation:

1. Reproduce the large picture cards for Little Miss Muffet on pages 4-7 to use with the whole class or a group of children.

2. Reproduce the activity sheet on page 8 for each child doing the activity. Children will need to cut the pictures apart before doing step three below.

Directions for Use:

1. Begin with the large cards. Hold up the first card of Little Miss Muffet and recite that line of the verse. Have students repeat it after you. Repeat this with each picture. When all the pictures are displayed in order, touch each one as you and the class recite the rhyme together.

2. Mix the cards up and pass them out to children. Have those children place the cards in the correct order. When the cards are in order, touch each picture as you recite the rhyme together.

3. Pass out the activity sheet. Have children cut the pictures apart. As the teacher recites each line of the verse, children put the pictures in the correct order in the boxes on the activity sheet.

4. Move around the room to check children's pictures. Have them paste the cards to their activity sheet in the correct order.

Additional Practice:

Follow the same procedure with the following rhymes.
- Humpty Dumpty (pages 9 - 12)
- Hey Diddle Diddle (pages 13 - 17)

Little Miss Muffet
Sat on a tuffet

4

Eating her curds and whey

Along came a spider
Who sat down beside her

6

And frightened
Miss Muffet away.

Sequencing • EMC 737

Note: Reproduce this page to use with the activity on page 3.

Name _____

Little Miss Muffet

✂ cut

🖊 paste

paste	paste	paste	paste

Sequencing • EMC 737

Humpty Dumpty
sat on a wall.

Humpty Dumpty had a great fall.

 Sequencing • EMC 737

All the king's horses

And all the king's men

Couldn't put Humpty

together again.

Note: Reproduce this page to use with the activity on page 3.

Name _____

Humpty Dumpty

✂ cut

paste

paste	paste	paste

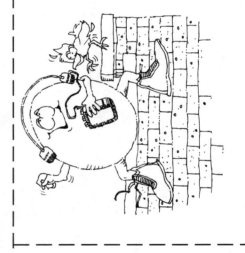

Hey Diddle Diddle
The cat and the fiddle

The cow jumped over the moon

 Sequencing • EMC 737

The little dog laughed
to see such a sight

And the dish ran away with the spoon.

 Sequencing • EMC 737

Name _____

Hey Diddle Diddle

✂ cut

paste

paste	paste	paste	paste

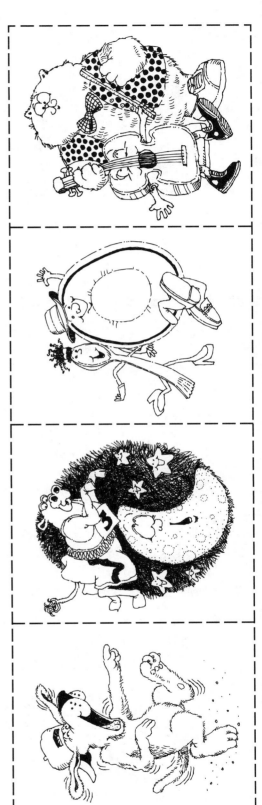

Sequencing Centers

table   **shelf**   **wall**

Materials for Centers:

You can use any of the reproducible sequencing activities in this book as center jobs. Follow these steps:

1. Reproduce the pictures or stories.

2. Color, laminate, and cut the tasks apart.

3. Put the pieces in an envelope or a self-closing plastic bag. Put a copy of one picture from the puzzle on the front of the envelope or bag so children replace the pieces in the correct container.

Sequencing puzzles purchased at educational bookstores or toy stores can also be placed in a sequencing center.

Center Storage:

Place the job envelopes in:
- a shoe box sitting on a table or shelf
- the pockets of a hanging shoe bag or card holder hanging on a wall

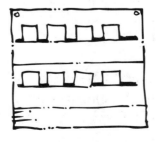

shoe box   **shoe bag**   **card holder**

                   Sequencing • EMC 737

Directions for Reproducible Sequencing Activities

Six types of reproducible sequencing activities are provided in the remainder of this book. Each type of activity has a numbered box logo. Use this as a guide for referring to pages 19 - 21 for teacher directions.

General Directions

These basic steps should be followed with any of the reproducible sequencing activities when the task is first introduced.

1. Discuss the pictures and/or words with children. (When working with the whole class, enlarge the pictures using a photocopier or make overhead transparencies of the pictures.) Discuss how the pictures or sentences should be arranged.

2. Have children cut out and arrange the pieces in the correct order. Have the teacher, aide, or a student partner check to see if the sequencing is correct.

3. Paste the pieces in place.

4. Review the completed sequence with students by asking students to describe orally what is happening in the story. Expand the activity by asking students what might happen after the final event in the story sequence.

Picture Stories

(pages 22 - 41)

Children are asked to sequence picture stories.
   three-part (pages 22 - 25)
   four-part (pages 26 - 31)
   six-part (pages 32 - 41)

The pictures are to be arranged so the "story" can be read from left to right. In order to do this with six-part stories, the pictures must be glued to the blank form provided. The boxes on the blank form are numbered 1-6 to avoid confusion.

         Sequencing • EMC 737

(pages 42-51)

This section contains two types of sequencing activities requiring children to determine what might happen next. One type asks children to select from pictures provided on the activity sheet; the other type asks children to draw their own pictures.

1. Cut and Paste (pages 42-46)
Each page contains pictures of three different events. Children "read" each picture, and then find a picture at the bottom of the page that shows what might happen next. The picture is to be cut out and pasted in the correct box. Each page contains one picture that will not be used.

You can extend the lesson by looking at the completed page and discussing other things that might have happened next.

2. Draw (pages 47-51)
These pages require children to "read" the picture to see what it contains (items or an event), then draw a picture to show what could happen next.

Some children may want to write what happens next. Invented spelling is okay at this stage of development.

3
Make a Sentence

(pages 52-61)

These pages are for children who have begun to read. The reading vocabulary is easy and sentence length varies from three to five words.

Children cut out the words and arrange them in a sequence that makes sense. First words and end punctuation are included to simplify the task.

On pages 52-61 picture clues are provided to help children arrange the sentences.

Extend the activity by asking children to read the sentences aloud to the teacher or a classmate.

(pages 62-81)

These four-part stories use both pictures and words to create the story. Most stories contain short vowel words and a few commonly used words (the, a, etc.). There are a few special words which will need to be introduced by the teacher. (In many cases the pictures and sentence content will give children all the clues they need to read the special words.)

Children cut out the sentences and paste them under the correct pictures to create a complete story.

Extend the activity by asking children to read the completed story aloud to the teacher or a classmate.

5
Sequence Stories

(pages 82-94)

These sequencing pages are for more able readers. There is only one picture to accompany the story, so there are less picture clues. The vocabulary contains both short and long vowel words and more special words.

Children cut out the sentences and glue them in an order that makes sense.

Extend the activity by asking children to read the completed story aloud to the teacher or a classmate.

6
Sequence and Write

(pages 95-106)

This type of activity is useful to help beginning writers sequence events when writing a story. Use three-part stories with beginners and four- and six-part stories with more advanced writers.

Reproduce the pictures and the writing form for each child.

Children cut out the pictures and glue them in order on the writing form. They then write a sentence about each picture.

At this stage of writing, spelling and punctuation should not be a major issue. Children are practicing writing events in sequence as preparation for more formal story writing as they get older.

When introducing these activity pages, you may want to discuss the pictures to elicit needed vocabulary. List these words on a chart or on the chalkboard for children to refer to while writing.

Name _____

Catch the Ball

✂ cut

🧴 paste

paste	paste	paste

Name

A Cat Grows

cut ✂ paste

paste

paste

paste

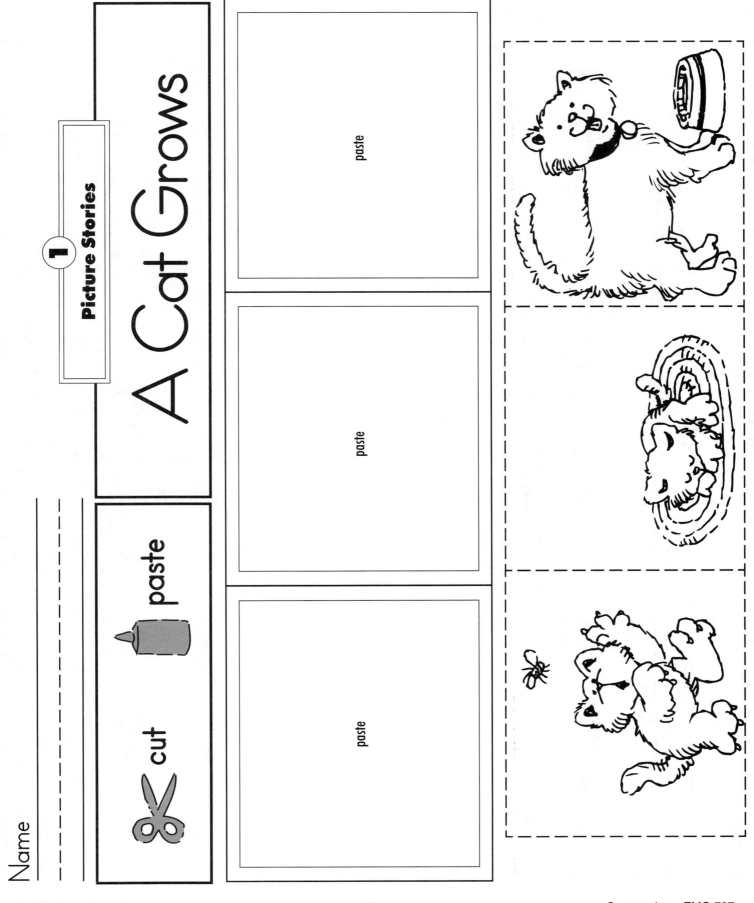

Name _____

Color Easter Eggs

✂ cut   🖊 paste

paste

paste

paste

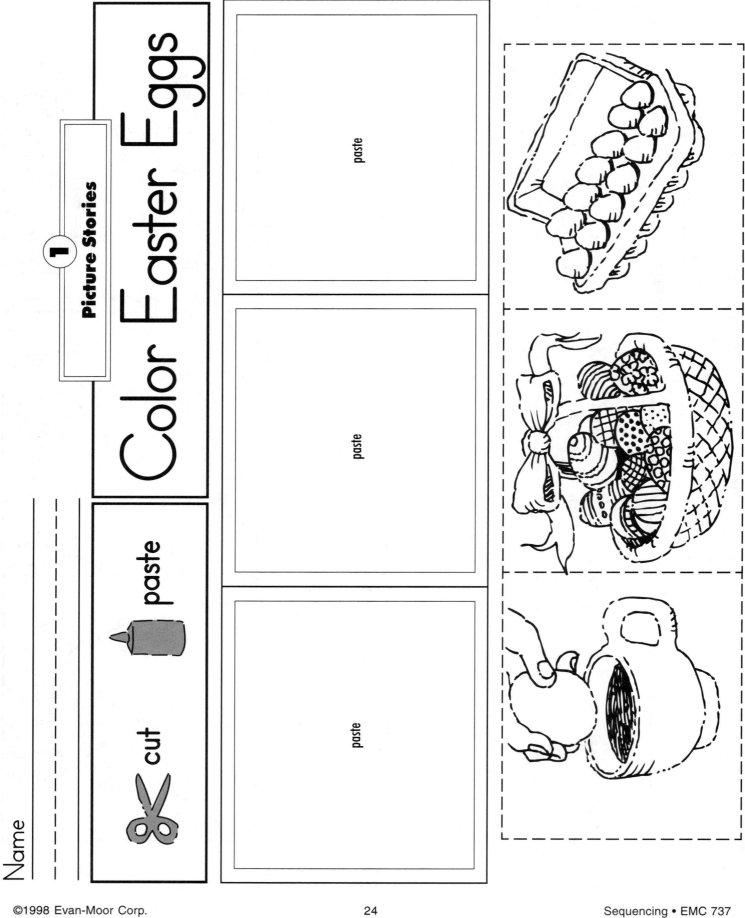

Name _____

Have a Banana

✂ cut   🖊 paste

paste

paste

paste

paste

paste

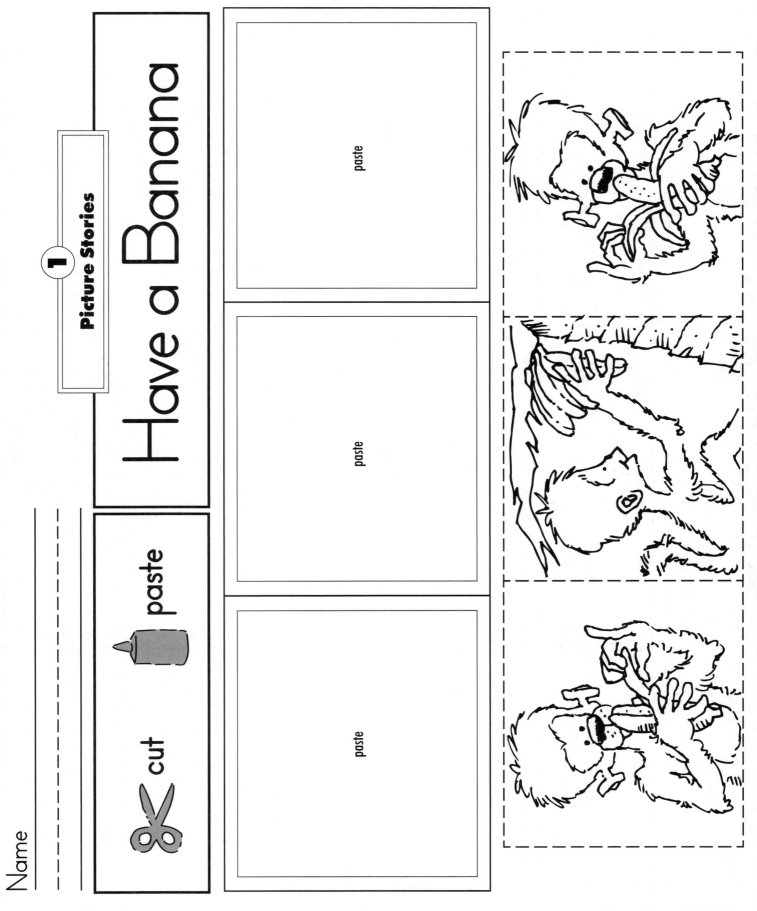

Birthday Cake

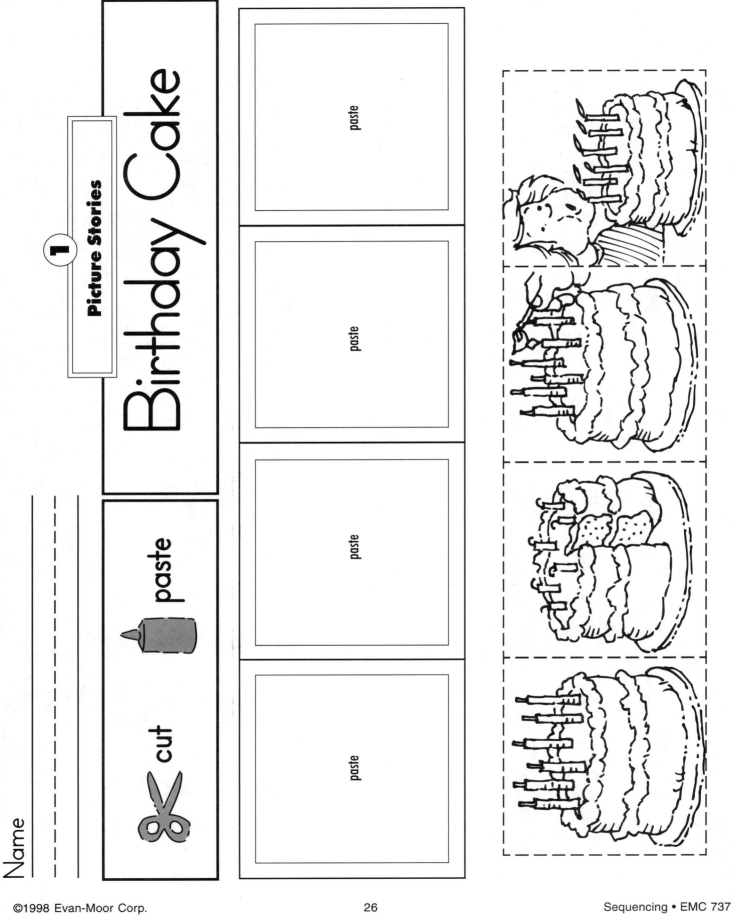

✂ cut

paste

paste

paste

paste

paste

Name _____

The Snowman

✂ cut   paste

paste	paste	paste	paste

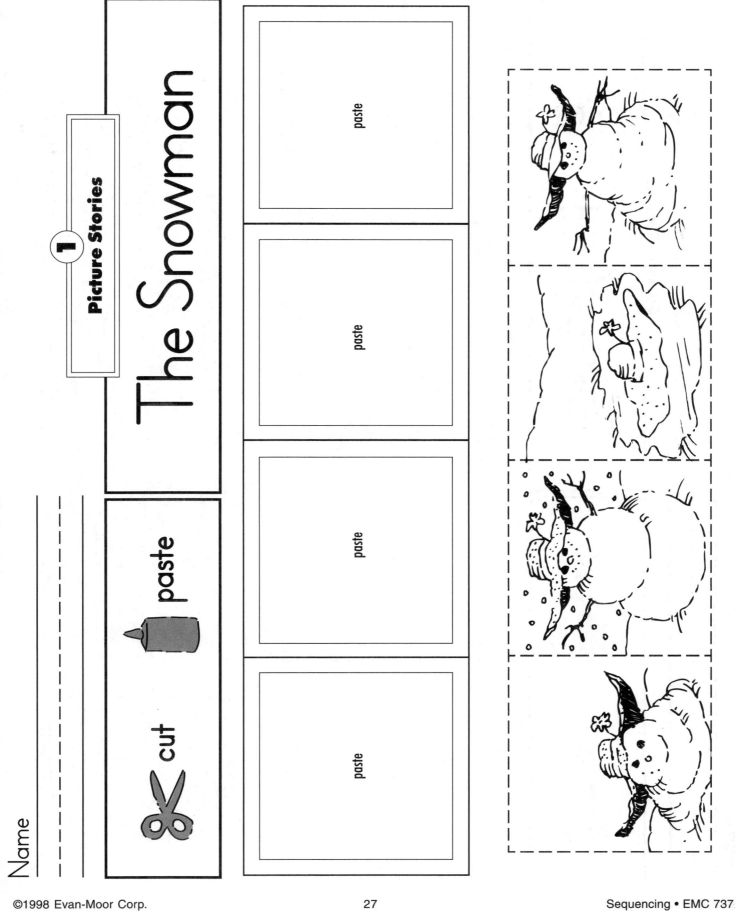

Name _____

Breakfast Time

✂ cut 🖍 paste

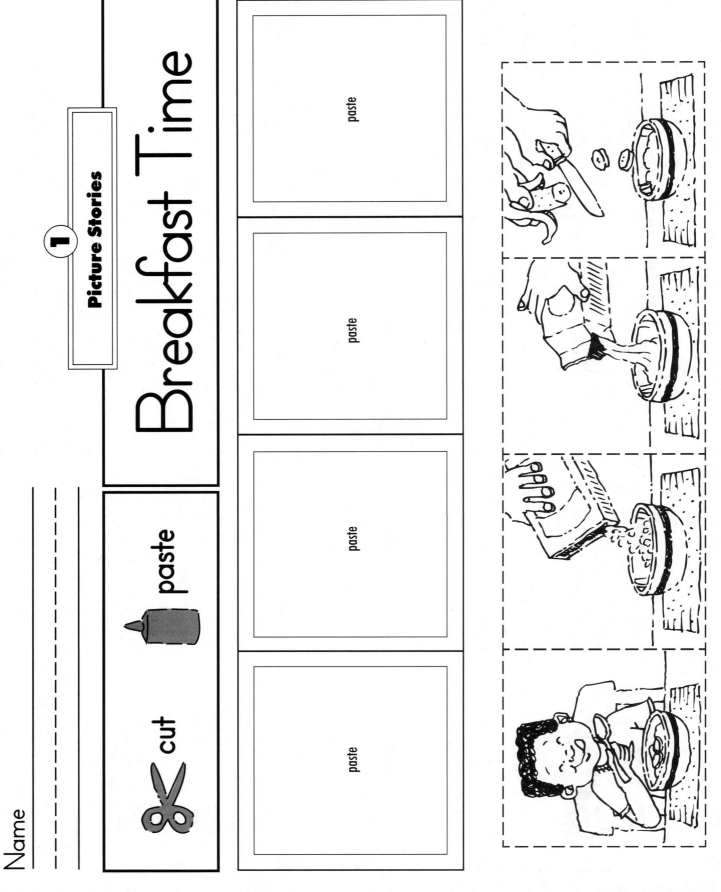

| paste | paste | paste | paste |

Name _____

Growing Corn

✂ cut   🗴 paste

paste	paste	paste	paste

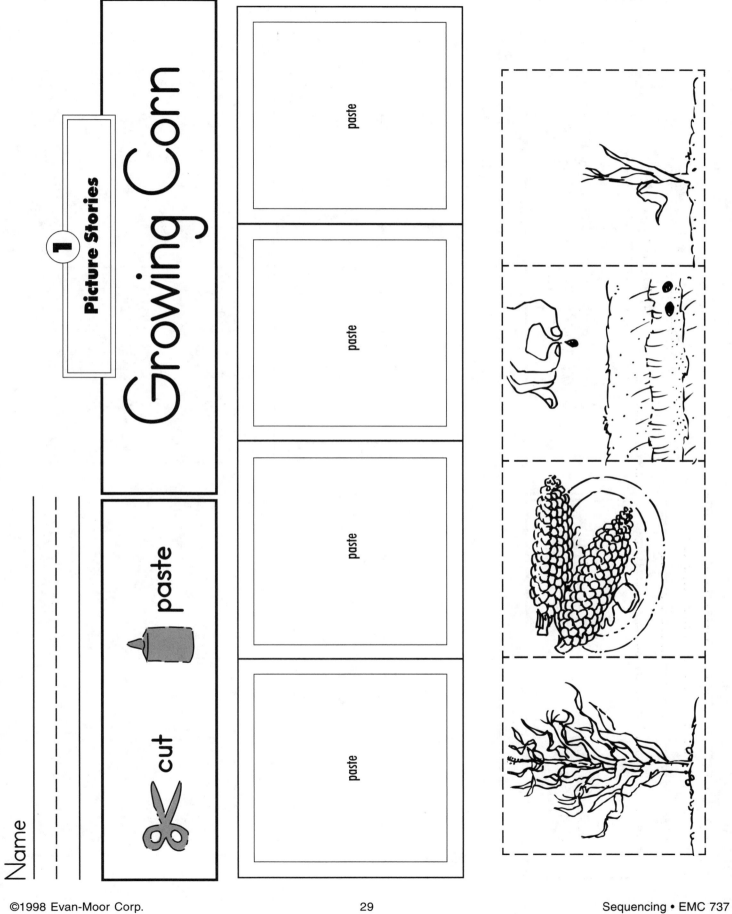

Name _____

Dog's Bath

✂ cut   paste

paste	paste	paste	paste

Name _____

Fly a Kite

paste

paste

paste

paste

✂ cut

paste

PARK

Name

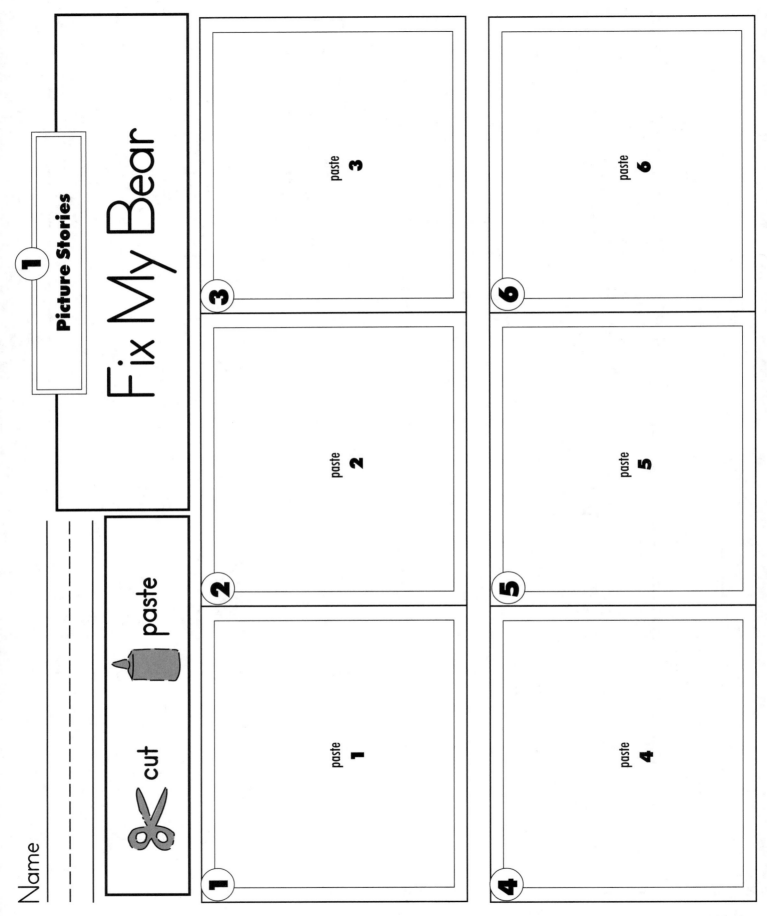

1 Picture Stories

Fix My Bear

cut paste

paste
1

paste
2

paste
3

paste
4

paste
5

paste
6

Fix My Bear

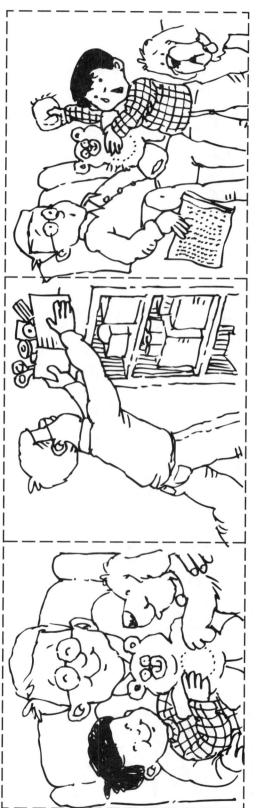

Name _____

A Butterfly Grows

✂ cut

paste

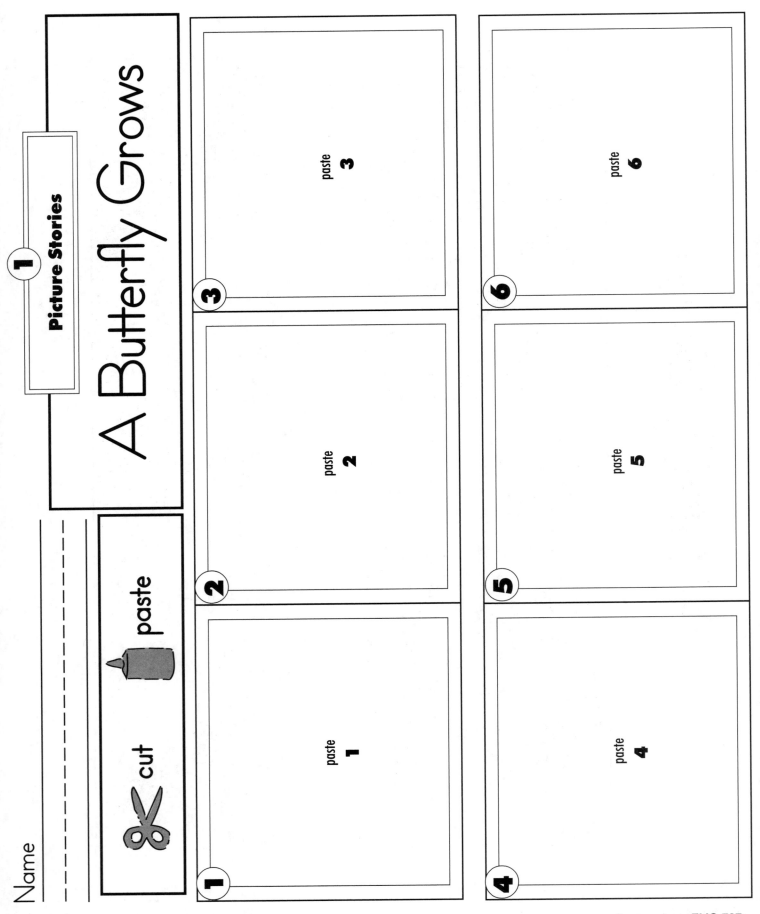

① paste 1

② paste 2

③ paste 3

④ paste 4

⑤ paste 5

⑥ paste 6

Sequencing • EMC 737

A Butterfly Grows

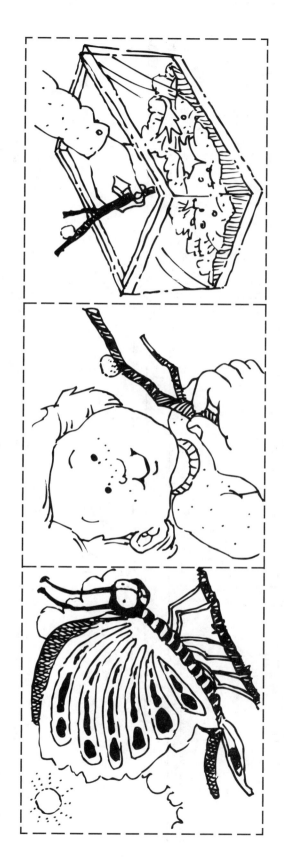

Name _____

Bake Cookies

cut ✂ | paste 🫙

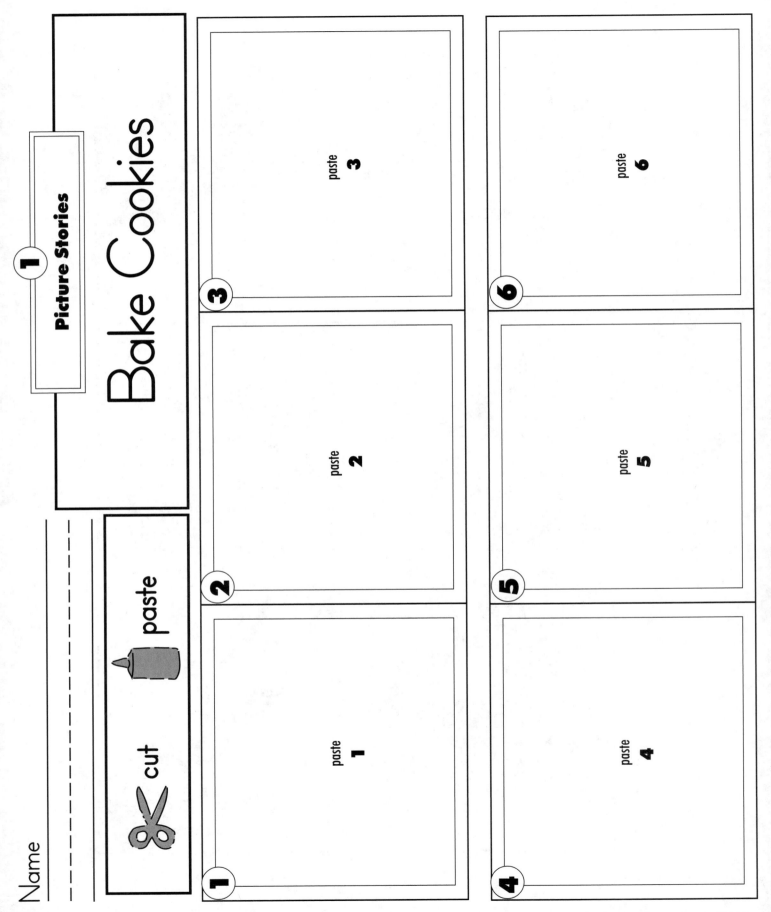

① paste 1	② paste 2	③ paste 3
④ paste 4	⑤ paste 5	⑥ paste 6

Bake Cookies

Name _____

Kim's Hair Wash

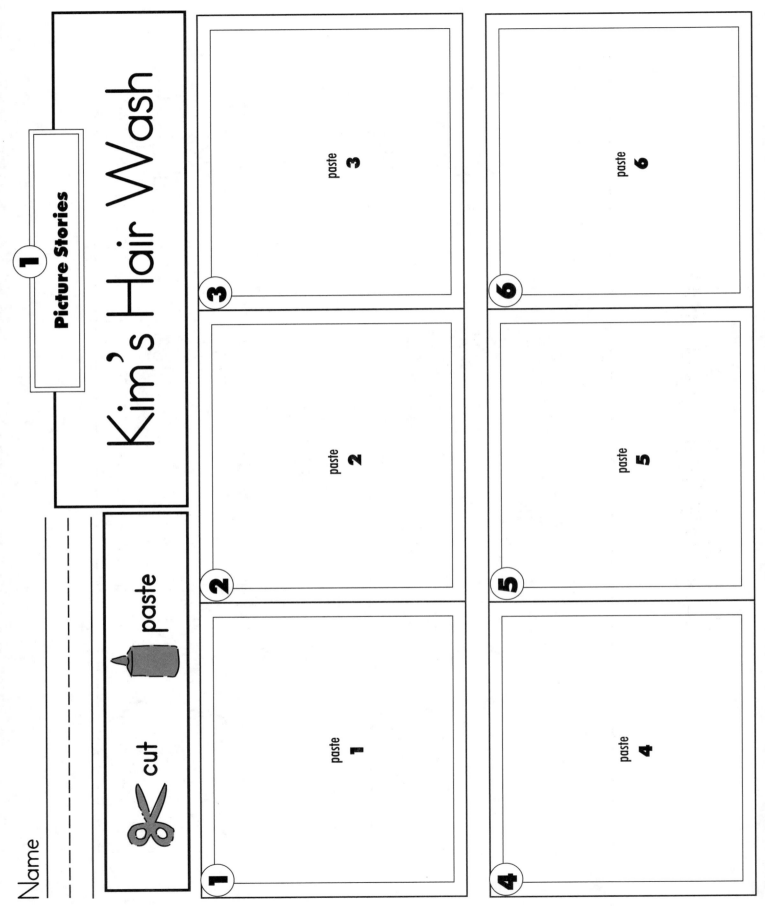

✂ cut   paste

① paste **1**

② paste **2**

③ paste **3**

④ paste **4**

⑤ paste **5**

⑥ paste **6**

Kim's Hair Wash

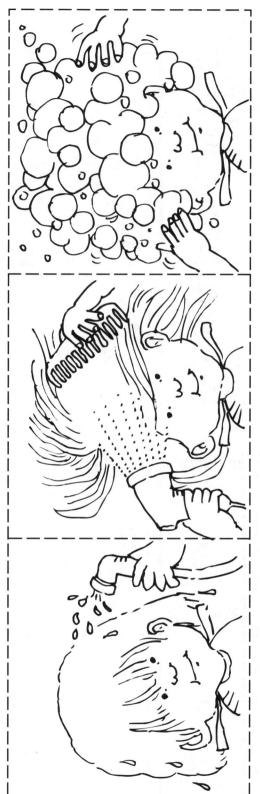

Sequencing • EMC 737

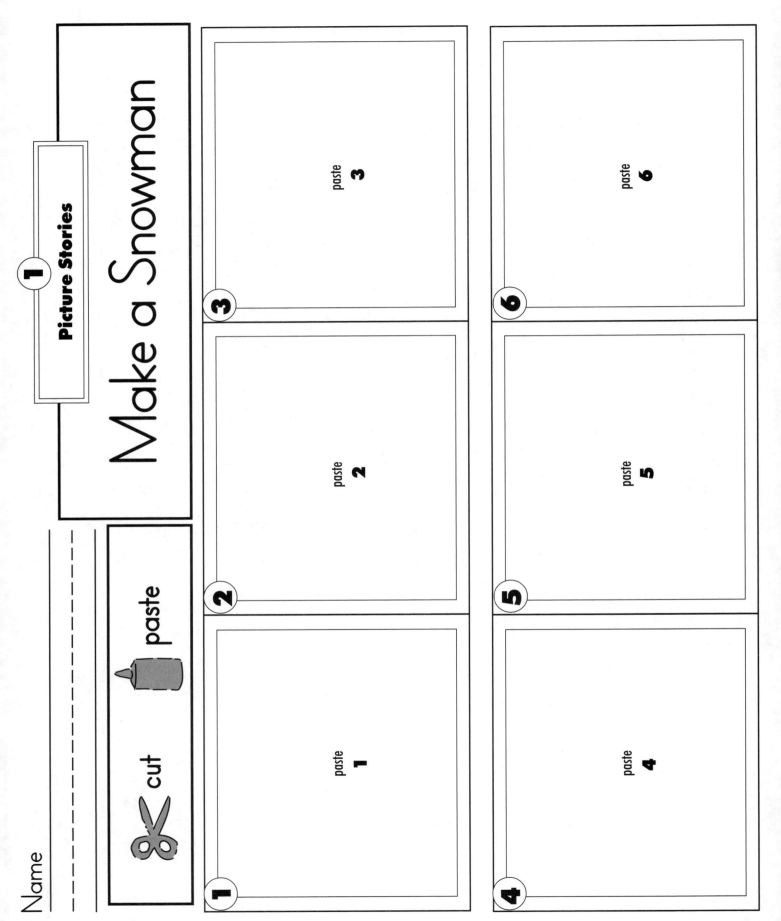

Make a Snowman

cut

paste

1 paste 1	**2** paste 2	**3** paste 3
4 paste 4	**5** paste 5	**6** paste 6

Make a Snowman

Sequencing • EMC 737

✂ cut   paste

paste

paste

paste

Sequencing • EMC 737

Name _____

✂ cut   🧴 paste

paste

paste

paste

Name _____

paste

paste

paste

Name

✂ cut   paste

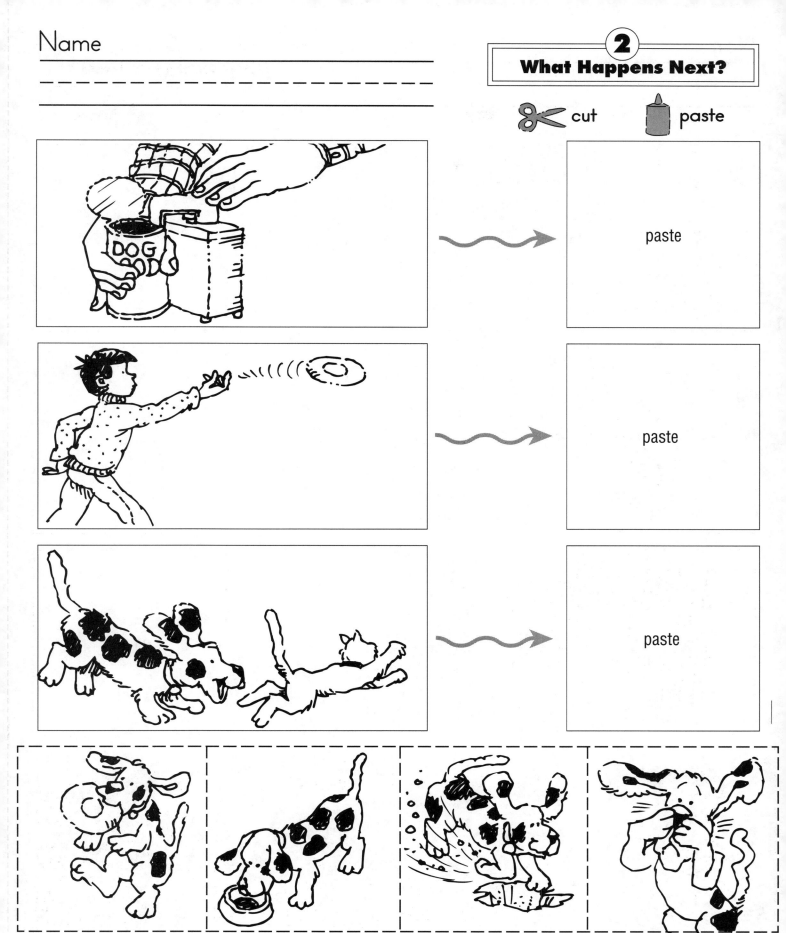

paste

paste

paste

✂ cut   ▮ paste

| | | paste |

| | | paste |

| | | paste |

Name _____

Name _____

Name _____

Name

Name

 cut paste

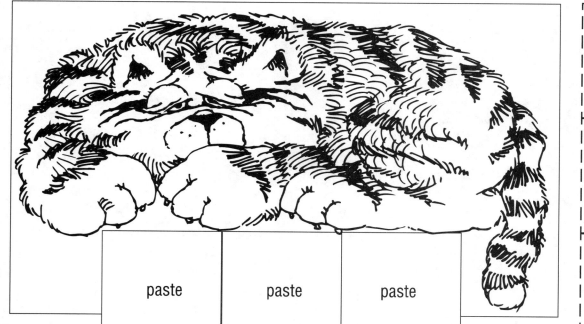

| paste | paste | paste |

the

Pet

cat.

| paste | paste | paste |

egg.

Get

an

52   Sequencing • EMC 737

Name _____

 cut paste

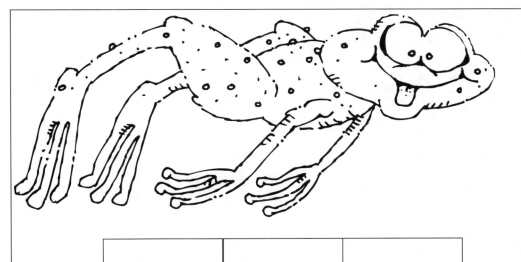

| paste | paste | paste |

hop.

can

I

| paste | paste | paste |

is

hot.

It

paste

cut

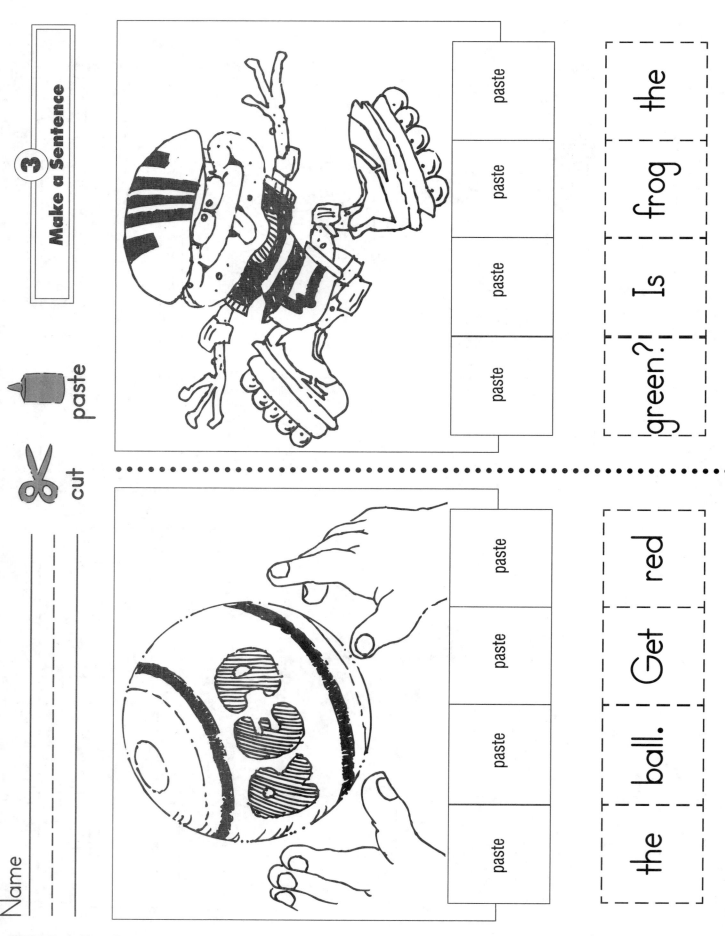

| paste | paste | paste | paste |

| the | Is | frog | the |

| paste | paste | paste | paste |

| the | Get | ball. | red |

Make a Sentence

Name

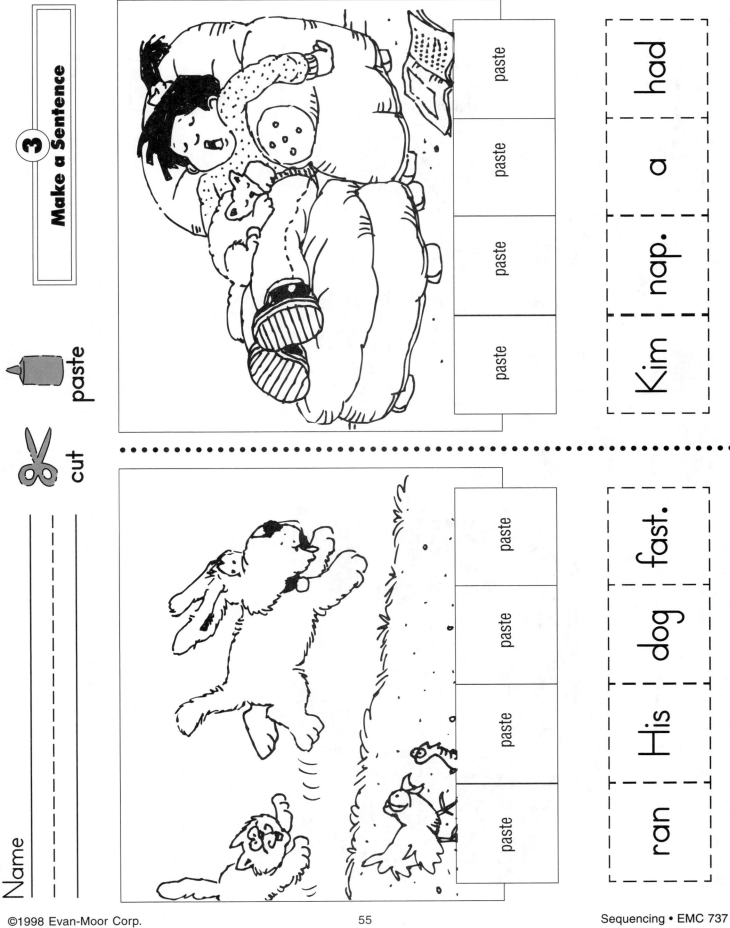

paste

cut

| paste | paste | paste | paste |

| had | a | nap. | Kim |

| paste | paste | paste | paste |

| fast. | dog | His | ran |

Sequencing • EMC 737

Name

✂ cut

paste

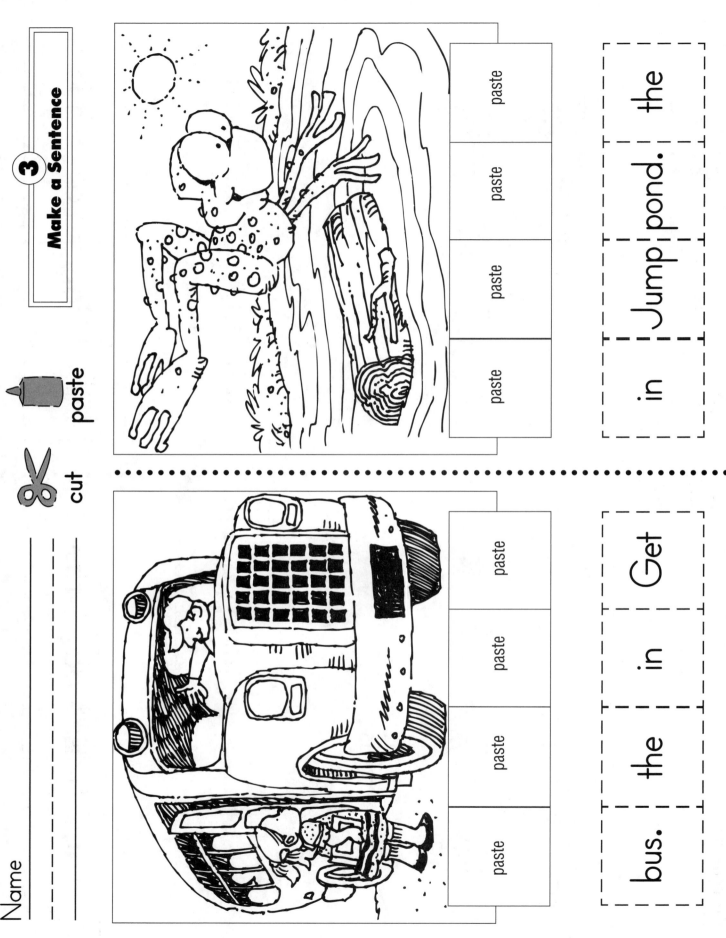

paste	paste	paste	paste

in | Jump | pond. | the

paste	paste	paste	paste

bus. | the | in | Get

Name

cut

paste

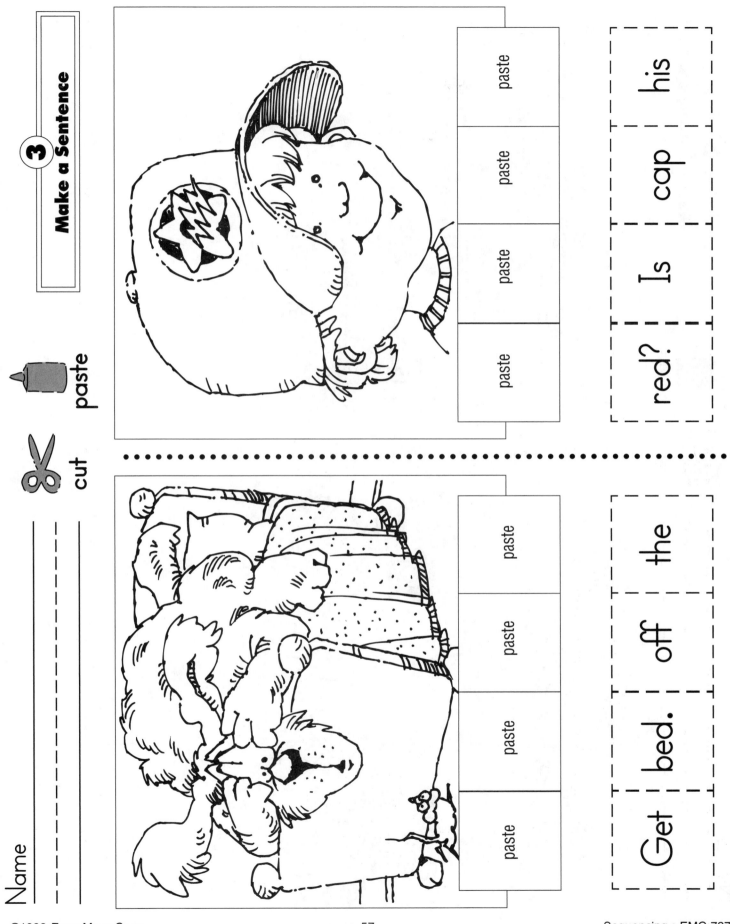

| paste | paste | paste | paste |

| his | cap | Is | red? |

| paste | paste | paste | paste |

| the | off | bed. | Get |

Sequencing • EMC 737

Name _____

✂ cut

paste

paste	paste	paste	paste	paste

Max | in | the | dug | mud.

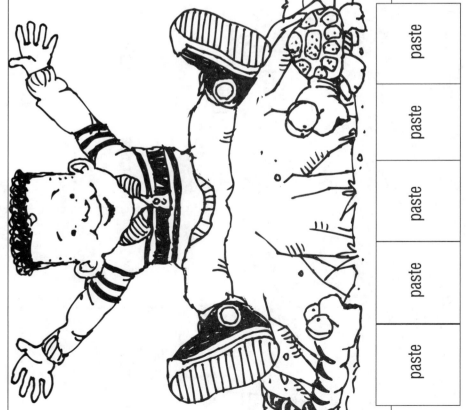

paste	paste	paste	paste	paste

sat | a | Tom | rock. | on

Sequencing • EMC 737

Name

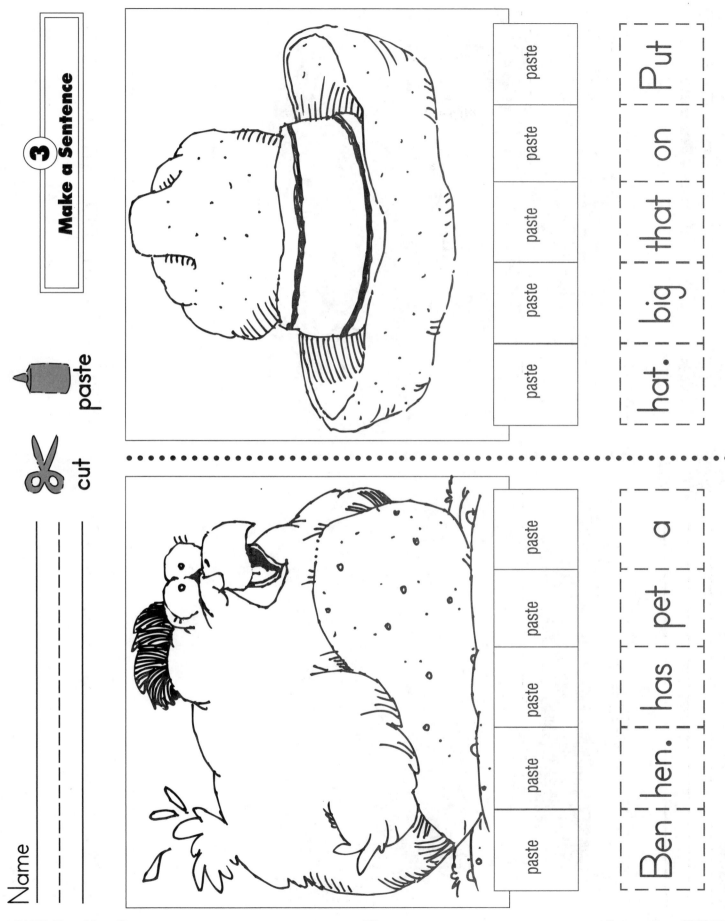

paste

cut

| paste | paste | paste | paste | paste |

Put | on | that | big | hat.

| paste | paste | paste | paste | paste |

Ben | has | pet | a

hen.

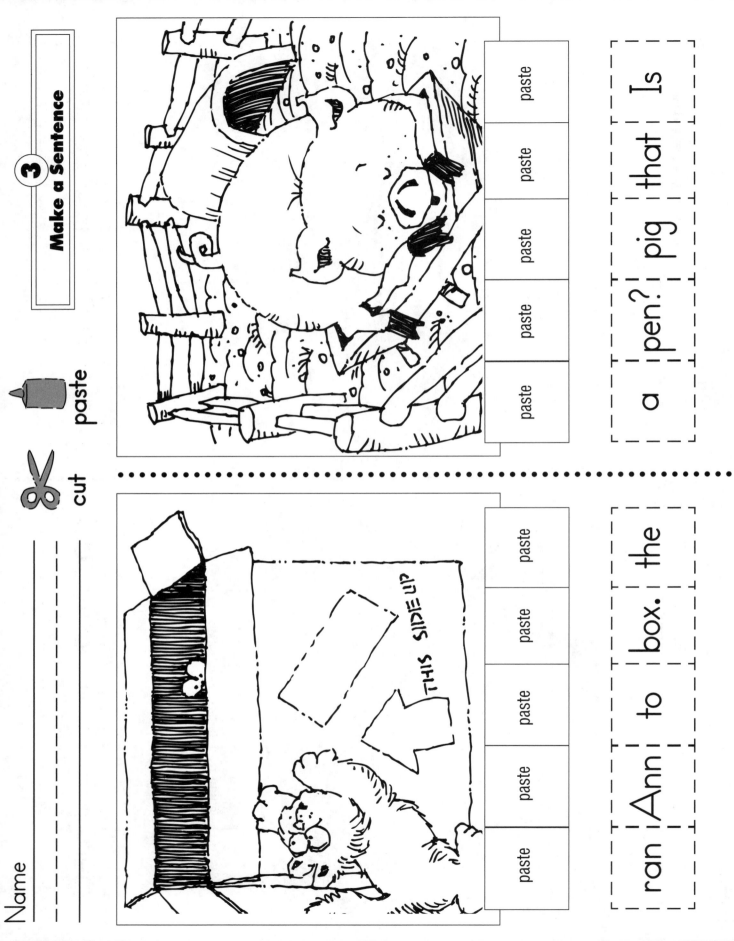

cut

paste

| paste | paste | paste | paste | paste |

| Is | that | pig | a | pen? |

| paste | paste | paste | paste | paste |

| the | box. | to | Ann | ran |

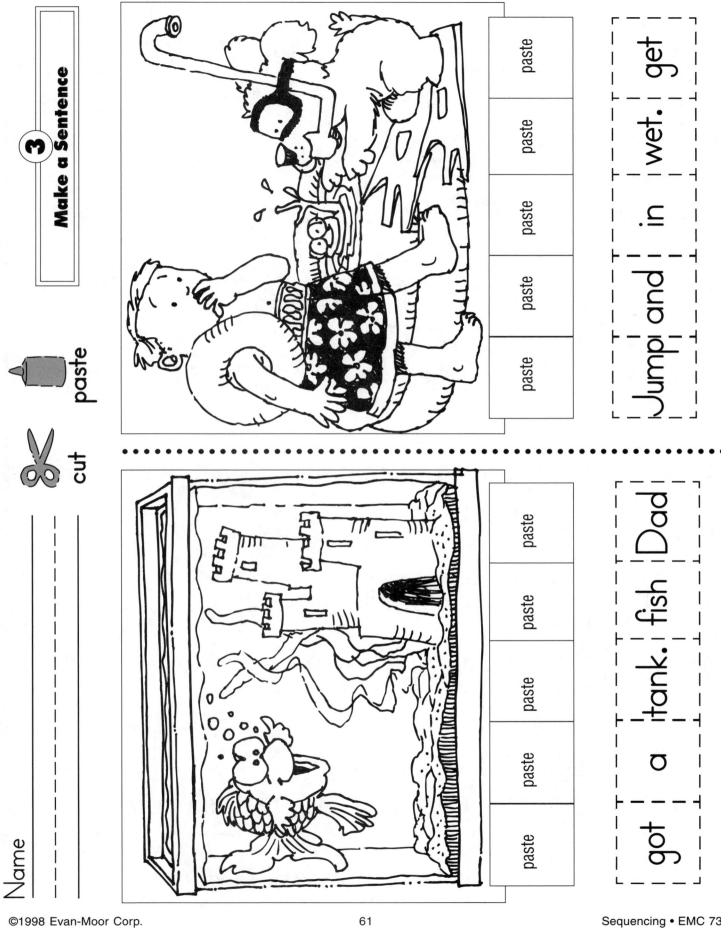

cut

paste

paste | paste | paste | paste | paste

Jump| and | in | wet. | get

paste | paste | paste | paste | paste

got | a | tank. | fish | Dad

Name _____

 cut paste

Ben's Cat

paste

paste

paste

paste

His cat gets a rat.

Ben has a pet cat.

Ben hugs his cat.

His cat sits on a mat.

Name

 cut ✂ paste

A Hot Day

paste

paste

paste

paste

| Let's go to the pond. | It is a hot day. |
| I am not hot now. | Jump in and get wet. |

Name _____

 cut paste

Get That Bug!

paste

paste

paste

paste

Max runs to get it.	A bug is in the grass.
Max did not get the bug.	Max sees the bug.

Sequencing • EMC 737

cut  paste

Blocks

paste

paste

paste

paste

Here I go.	2 blocks.
I block.	3 blocks.

Name _____

✂ cut   paste

Fun in the Mud

paste

paste

paste

paste

Tim is a mess. He must get a bath. | Tim had a bath. He is not a mess.

Tim sat in the mud. | Tim dug in the mud. He had fun.

Sequencing • EMC 737

Name _____

Camp

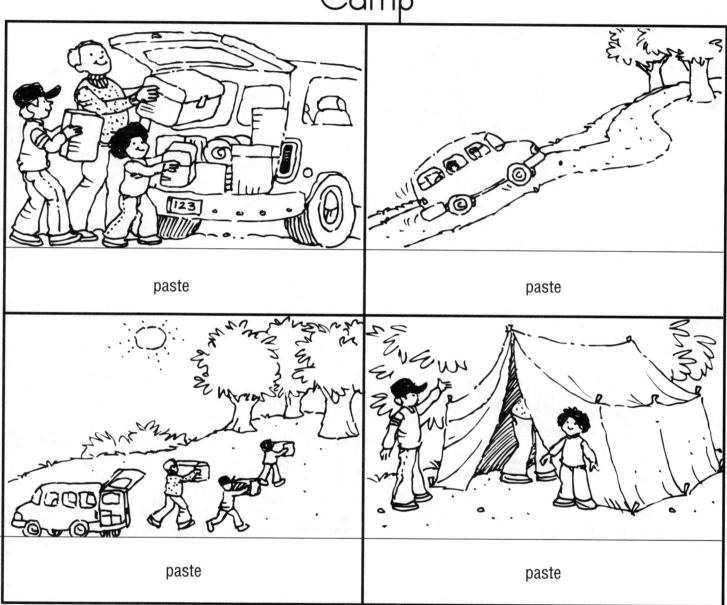

paste	paste
paste	paste

It is fun to camp.	Go up the hills to the camp.
Pack the car.	Unpack the car. Set up the tent.

Name _____

 cut paste

Hats

| paste | paste |
| paste | paste |

| Tim got a flat hat. | Let's get to the tent. It's time to begin. |
| Bob got a big hat. | Jill got a small hat. |

Name

 cut paste

Fix the Dent

paste

paste

paste

paste

| Ann's wagon is bent. | Ann hit a stump. |
| Dad did fix the dent.
The wagon is not bent. | Can Dad fix the dent? |

69   Sequencing • EMC 737

Nap Time

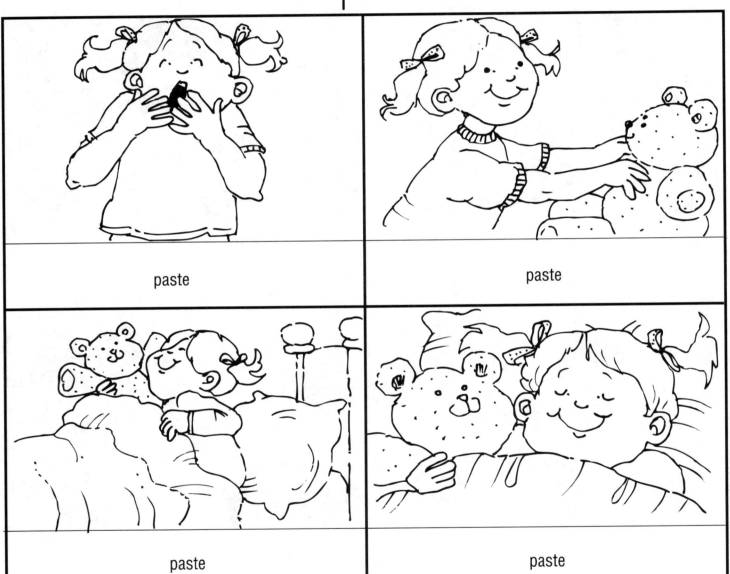

paste

paste

paste

paste

| Pam got Ted. | Pam went to sleep. |
| It is nap time. | Pam got in bed. |

Name _____

Name _____

 cut   paste

Hop, Hop, Hop

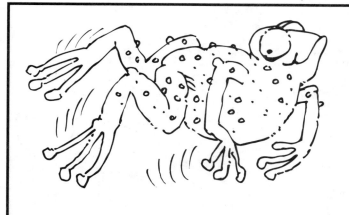

paste

paste

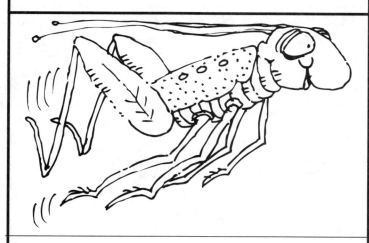

paste

paste

| Can you hop too? | Grasshoppers hop. |
| Frogs hop. | Kangaroos hop. |

Name _____

 cut  paste

Circus Fun

paste

paste

paste

paste

| Pat grinned. Ken clapped. | It is fun to be at the circus. |
| Pat and Ken sat on a bench. | Pat and Ken got tickets. |

Sequencing • EMC 737

Box Car

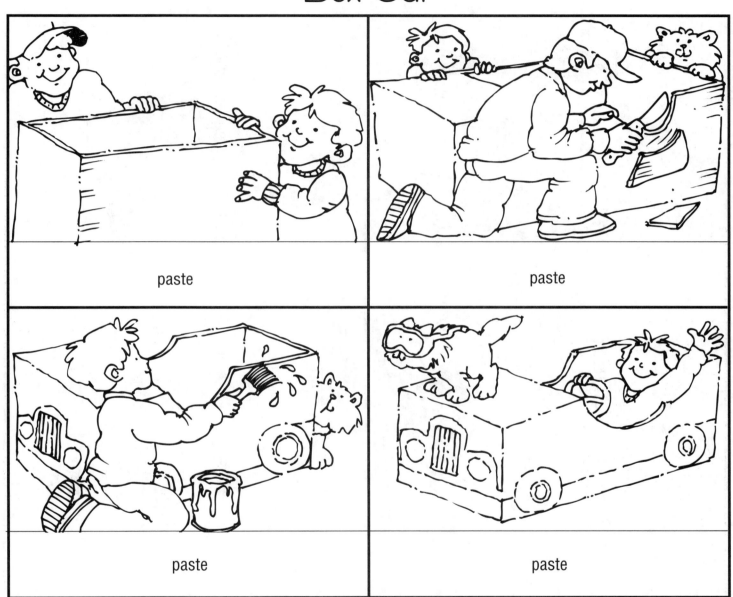

paste

paste

paste

paste

Cut.	Get in and ride.
Paint.	Get a box.

 cut   paste

What a Mess!

paste

paste

paste

paste

| It's not a mess now. | What a mess! |
| Pick up the toys. | Make the bed. |

Name _____

 cut  paste

Get the Mouse

paste

paste

paste

paste

| The mouse ran. | I got it at last! |
| Eek, a mouse! | I ran to get a net. |

cut  paste

An Ant Can't

paste

paste

paste

paste

An ant can't hop. But I can.

An ant can't swim. But I can.

But an ant can eat. And so can I.

An ant can't sing. But I can.

Sequencing • EMC 737

Name _____

 cut  paste

A Snack for Frog

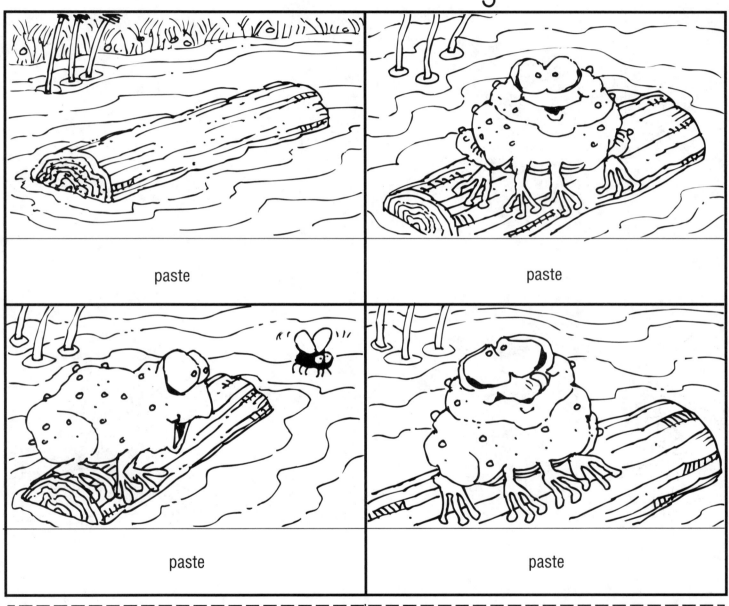

paste	paste
paste	paste

Frog did get the bug. Yum!	A log is in the pond.
Frog sees a fat, black bug. Can he get the bug?	A big green frog sits on the log.

 cut paste

Pet Pig

paste

paste

paste

paste

| Kim has a pet pig. Pig is in its pen. | Pig is back in its pen. |
| Pig gets away. Pig runs and runs. | Stop, Pig, stop! Kim gets the pig. |

Name _____

 cut   paste

My Black Hen

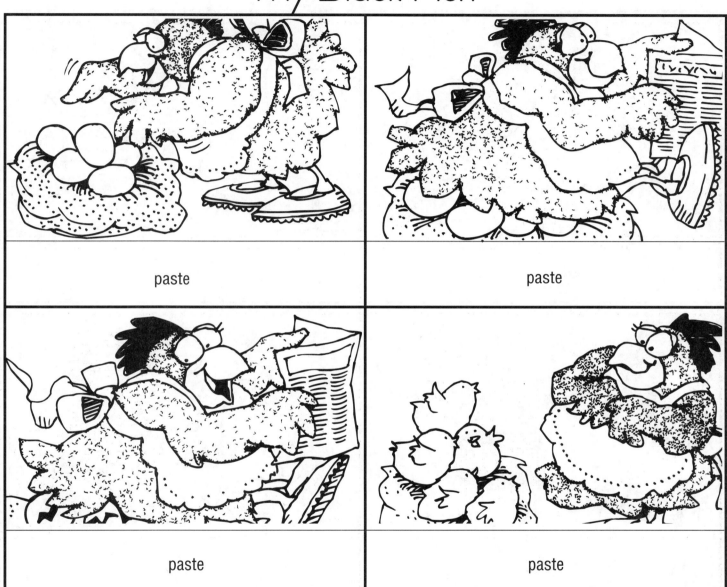

paste   paste

paste   paste

| Can you see cracks in the eggs? | My black hen has five chicks. |
| My black hen sat on the eggs. | My black hen put five eggs in the nest. |

Name _____

 cut paste

Gift Box

paste

paste

paste

paste

| Max set the box on the step. What is in the box? | A jet is in the box. A jet for Ron. |
| Ron got the box. What is in the box? | "Pick up the lid, Ron." What is in the box? |

Name _____

 cut   paste

A Pet Puppy

paste

paste

paste

paste

Jill and Mom went to the pet shop.	Jill and the puppy are happy.
Jill got a puppy.	Jill asked for a pet.

81

Name _____

Sequence Stories

 cut   paste

Ed Egg

| 1 |
| 2 |
| 3 |
| 4 |

| Ed is sad. His shell has a crack. | Ed sat on a rock. |
| Ed fell off the rock. | Mom Egg and Dad Egg picked Ed up. |

82   Sequencing • EMC 737

Name _____

 cut   paste

Lunch Time

| 1 |
| 2 |
| 3 |
| 4 |

| Last, I fed my lizard a bug. | Now I can eat my lunch. |
| First, I fed my bird seeds. | Next, I fed my dog a bone. |

83   Sequencing • EMC 737

Name _____

 cut  paste

A Note

1
2
3
4

Pam asked her mom. Mom said, "Yes."	Pam got a note.
It was from Jill.	The note said, "Can you sleep at my house?"

Name _____

 cut   paste

Feed the Dog

1

2

3

4

Put dog food in the dish.	Open the sack.
Get the sack of dog food and a dish.	Call your dog.

Name _____

 cut   paste

Fun at the Pond

| 1 |
| 2 |
| 3 |
| 4 |

| Tasha jumps in the pond. | She pulls with her arms. |
| Tasha likes to swim. | She kicks with her legs. |

Name _____

 cut   paste

Stuck

1	
2	
3	
4	
5	
6	

He ran to the box.	B. J. went in the box.
B. J. saw a big box.	Gus got B. J. out of the box.
"Help! I can't get out," yelled B. J.	B. J. gave Gus a big hug.

5
Sequence Stories

✂ cut paste

The First Day of School

1	
2	
3	
4	
5	
6	

First, get dressed.	Find the room.
Meet the teacher.	Wake up.
Ride the bus.	Then eat breakfast.

 Sequencing • EMC 737

Name

Make a Puppet

	1
	2
	3
	4
	5
	6

What will the puppet say?	First, make puppet eyes.
Second, make a puppet nose.	Then make a funny mouth.
Get a bag and marking pens.	Put a hand in the bag.

✂ cut paste

A Fish for Pam

1	
2	
3	
4	
5	
6	

He put the fish in its tank.	Dad got a goldfish for Pam.
She went to the pet shop with her dad.	Pam fed her pet. "I like my fish," she said.
"I wish I had a fish," said Pam.	Dad got a tank for the fish.

     Sequencing • EMC 737

Name _____

 cut paste

Skates

	1
	2
	3
	4
	5
	6

Lee got up.	Plop. Lee fell down.
He put them on.	Lee got skates.
He skated again.	Skate, Lee.

©1998 Evan-Moor Corp.   91   Sequencing • EMC 737

Name _____

 cut paste

Let's Go!

	1
	2
	3
	4
	5
	6

Carlos ran fast.	He got his black shoes.
He ran to the park.	He put on the socks – 1, 2.
Carlos got his red socks.	He put on the shoes – 1, 2.

Sequencing • EMC 737

Name _____

 cut    paste

The Three Bears

	1
	2
	3
	4
	5
	6

She went to sleep in baby bear's bed.	The three bears went for a walk.
Goldilocks went into the house.	She ate baby bear's porridge all up.
The bears came back. Goldilocks ran away.	Then she broke baby bear's chair.

cut   paste

Hot Chocolate

1	
2	
3	
4	
5	
6	

Put chocolate in the milk.	Put the milk in the pan.
Drink it up.	Put the hot chocolate in a cup.
Put the pan on the stove.	Mix up the chocolate and milk.

   Sequencing • EMC 737

Name

 cut paste  write

A Snack

paste	_____
	_____
	_____
paste	_____
	_____
	_____
paste	_____
	_____
	_____

Sequencing • EMC 737

Be a Clown

paste	
paste	
paste	

Name _____

 cut  paste write

Up and Down

paste	_____
	_____
paste	_____
	_____
paste	_____
	_____

Name _____

 cut paste write

Apple Pie

paste	_____
paste	
paste	
paste	

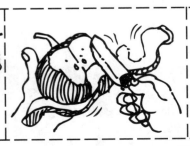  

Sequencing • EMC 737

Name _____

cut   paste   write

Toast for Breakfast

paste	_____
paste	_____
paste	_____
paste	_____

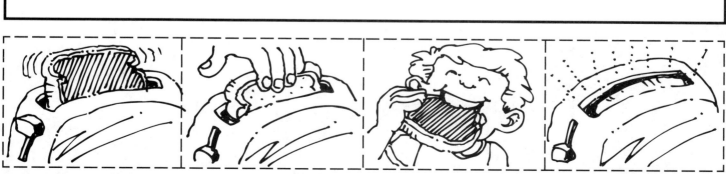

Name

 cut paste write

Get a Hit

paste	_____
paste	_____
paste	_____
paste	_____

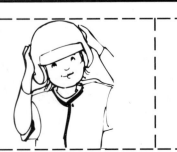  

Name _____

6 Sequence and Write

cut   paste   write

Making a Garden

paste	_____
paste	_____
paste	_____
paste	_____

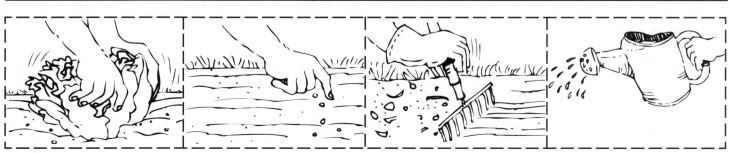

101   Sequencing • EMC 737

Name _____

Pickle and Ham Sandwich

paste	
paste	
paste	
paste	

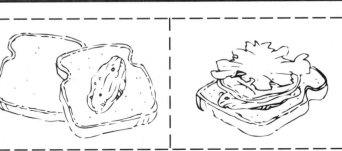

Note: Reproduce pages 105 and 106 to sequence and write about these pictures.

 ✂ cut 🍶 paste ✏ write

6 Sequence and Write

Note: Reproduce pages 105 and 106 to sequence and write about these pictures.

 cut  paste write

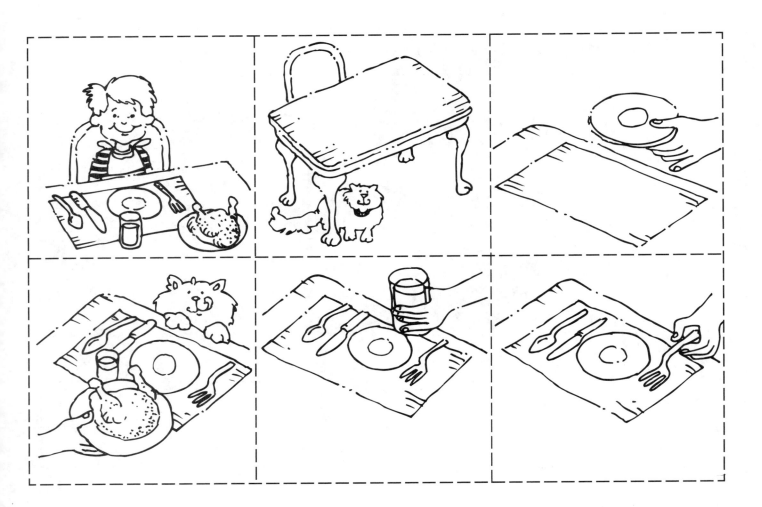

Note: Reproduce pages 105 and 106 to use with the pictures on pages 103 and 104.

Name

1

paste

_____

_____

_____

_____

2

paste

_____

_____

_____

3

paste

_____

_____

_____

4

paste	_____
	_____
	_____
	_____

5

paste	_____
	_____
	_____
	_____

6

paste	_____
	_____
	_____
	_____

Answer Key

Page 8
Child sitting surrounded by animals
Child eating
Spider appears
Child runs

Page 12
Humpty on wall
Humpty falling
Humpty with horse & soldier

Page 17
Cat & fiddle
Cow jumping over moon
Dog laughing
Dish & spoon

Page 22
Boy throws ball
Dog chases ball
Dog catches ball

Page 23
Kitten on rug
Larger kitten chasing bug
Grown cat at food dish

Page 24
Carton of eggs
Dipping egg in cup
Colored eggs in basket

Page 25
Picking banana
Beginning to peel banana
Banana mostly peeled

Page 26
Cake with candles
Lighting candles
Blowing out candles
Cake with piece missing

Page 27
Snowman in snow
Snowman beginning to melt
Snowman with only head left
Puddle with hat

Page 28
Pouring cereal
Slicing banana
Pouring milk
Eating cereal

Page 29
Planting seeds
Small corn plant
Large corn plant
Corn on plate

Page 30
Dirty dog (picture 1 & 2 could be reversed)
Tub being filled
Dog in tub
Clean dog

Page 31
Taking kite out of box
Walking to park
Running with kite
Kite flying

Page 32
Boy & dog pull on bear
Arm comes off bear
Crying boy goes to man
Man gets box of sewing supplies
Man sews arm back on
Happy characters with bear

Page 34

    Boy with branch with egg on it

    Putting branch in container

    Caterpillar on branch

    Branch with cocoon

    Butterfly on branch

    Butterfly flies out window

Page 36

    Pouring flour

    Mixing with spoon

    Spooning dough on cookie tray

    Putting tray on oven (cookies irregular shape)

    Taking cookies out of oven (cookies round)

    Eating a cookie

Page 38

    Girl with untidy hair

    Wetting hair

    Lathering hair

    Towel-drying hair

    Blow-drying hair

    Clean hair with bow

Page 40

    Rolling snowballs

    Stacking second ball

    Stacking third ball

    Adding stick arms

    Adding nose

    Adding hat

Page 42

    child with tire pump

    sand castle

    child brushing teeth

Page 43

    bouquet of flowers

    short grass

    hand picking carrot

Page 44

    bringing home groceries

    painting fence

    wearing paper mask

Page 45

    dog eating dinner

    dog catching frisbee

    dog holding nose

Page 46

    child playing in snow

    child walking in rain

    child playing in sun

Page 47

    Pictures will vary—-should show in some way:

    a sandwich

    a glass of chocolate milk

    popped popcorn

Page 48

    Pictures will vary—should show in some way:

    an inflated balloon

    dog finding something in the hole OR dog being scolded

    a gift box

Page 49

    Pictures will vary—should show in some way:

    a plant growing in a pot

    a baby animal just out of its egg

    a blooming flower

Page 50

Pictures will vary—should show in some way:
child in bed
child with bandage on leg
bird flying away OR bird in cage with door shut

Page 51

Pictures will vary—should show in some way:
child playing in snow
magician pulling something out of the hat
child catching fish

Page 52

Pet the cat.
Get an egg.

Page 53

I can hop.
It is hot.

Page 54

Get the red ball.
Is the frog green?

Page 55

His dog ran fast.
Kim had a nap.

Page 56

Get in the bus.
Jump in the pond.

Page 57

Get off the bed.
Is his cap red?

Page 58

Tom sat on a rock.
Max dug in the mud.

Page 59

Ben has a pet hen.
Put on that big hat.

Page 60

Ann ran to the box.
Is that a pig pen?

Page 61

Jump in and get wet.
Dad got a fish tank.

Page 62

Ben has a pet cat.
His cat sits on a mat.
His cat gets a rat.
Ben hugs his cat.

Page 63

It is a hot day.
Let's go to the pond.
Jump in and get wet.
I am not hot now.

Page 64

A bug is in the grass.
Max sees the bug.
Max runs to get it.
Max did not get the bug.

Page 65

1 block.
2 blocks.
3 blocks.
Here I go.

Page 66

Tim sat in the mud.
Tim dug in the mud. He had fun.
Tim is a mess. He must get a bath.
Tim had a bath. He is not a mess.

Page 67

Pack the car.
Go up the hills to the camp.
Unpack the car. Set up the tent.
It is fun to camp.

Page 68

Bob got a big hat.

Jill got a small hat.

Tim got a flat hat.

Let's get to the tent. It's time to begin.

Page 69

Ann hit a stump.

Ann's wagon is bent.

Can Dad fix the dent?

Dad did fix the dent. The wagon is not bent.

Page 70

It is nap time.

Pam got Ted.

Pam got in bed.

Pam went to sleep.

Page 71

Frogs hop.

Kangaroos hop.

Grasshoppers hop.

Can you hop too?

Page 72

Pat and Ken got tickets.

Pat and Ken sat on a bench.

Pat grinned.Ken clapped.

It is fun to be at the circus.

Page 73

Get a box.

Cut.

Paint.

Get in and ride.

Page 74

What a mess!

Pick up the toys.

Make the bed.

It's not a mess now.

Page 75

Eek, a mouse.

The mouse ran.

I ran to get a net.

I got it at last!

Page 76

An ant can't hop. But I can.

An ant can't sing. But I can.

An ant can't swim. But I can.

But an ant can eat. And so can I.

Page 77

A log is in the pond.

A big green frog sits on the log.

Frog sees a fat, black bug. Can he get the bug?

Frog did get the bug. Yum!

Page 78

Kim has a pet pig. Pig is in its pen.

Pig gets away. Pig runs and runs.

Stop, Pig, stop! Kim gets the pig.

Pig is back in its pen.

Page 79

My black hen put five eggs in the nest.

My black hen sat on the eggs.

Can you see cracks in the eggs?

My black hen has five chicks.

Page 80

Max set the box on the step.

What is in the box?

Ron got the box.

What is in the box?

"Pick up the lid, Ron."

What is in the box?

A jet is in the box.

A jet for Ron.

Page 81

Jill asked for a pet.
Jill and Mom went to the pet shop.
Jill got a puppy.
Jill and the puppy are happy.

Page 82

Ed sat on a rock.
Ed fell off the rock.
Mom Egg and Dad Egg picked Ed up.
Ed is sad.
His shell has a crack.

Page 83

First, I fed my bird seeds.
Next, I fed my dog a bone.
Last, I fed my lizard a bug.
Now I can eat my lunch.

Page 84

Pam got a note.
It was from Jill.
The note said, "Can you sleep at my house?"
Pam asked her mom. Mom said, "Yes."

Page 85

Get the sack of dog food and a dish.
Open the sack.
Put dog food in the dish.
Call your dog.

Page 86

Tasha jumps in the pond.
She kicks with her legs.
She pulls with her arms.
Tasha likes to swim. (could also be first)

Page 87

B. J. saw a big box.
He ran to the box.
B. J. went in the box.
"Help! I can't get out," yelled B. J.
Gus got B. J. out of the box.
B. J. gave Gus a big hug.

Page 88

Wake up.
First, get dressed.
Then eat breakfast.
Ride the bus.
Find the room.
Meet the teacher.

Page 89

Get a bag and marking pens.
First, make puppet eyes.
Second, make a puppet nose.
Then make a funny mouth.
Put a hand in the bag.
What will the puppet say?

Page 90

"I wish I had a fish," said Pam.
She went to the pet shop with her dad.
Dad got a goldfish for Pam.
Dad got a tank for the fish.
He put the fish in its tank.
Pam fed her pet.
"I like my fish," she said.

Page 91

Lee got skates.
He put them on.
Skate, Lee. (could be last also)
Plop. Lee fell down.
Lee got up.
He skated again.

Page 92

Carlos got his red socks.
He got his black shoes.
He put on the sox—1, 2.
He put on the shoes—1, 2.
Carlos ran fast.
He ran to the park.

Page 93

The three bears went for a walk.

Goldilocks went into the house.

She ate baby bear's porridge all up.

Then she broke baby bear's chair.

She went to sleep in baby bear's bed.

The bears came back.

Goldilocks ran away.

Page 94

Put the milk in the pan.

Put chocolate in the milk.

Mix up the chocolate and milk.

Put the pan on the stove.

Put the hot chocolate in a cup.

Drink it up.

Page 95

Getting box

Inserting straw

Drinking

Page 96

Putting on makeup

Putting on nose

Putting on wig

Page 97

Climbing up ladder

Sliding down

In a heap at bottom

Page 98

Peeling apples

Slicing apples

Pie in oven

Piece of pie on plate

Page 99

Putting bread in toaster

Bread toasting

Toast popped up

Eating toast

Page 100

Putting on helmet

Ready to bat

Running

Reaching base

Page 101

Raking dirt

Planting seeds

Watering

Picking lettuce

Page 102

Bread with pickle

Bread with meat on pickle

Bread with lettuce added

Finished sandwich

Page 103

Picking pumpkin

Paying for pumpkin

Cutting off top

Scooping out seeds

Carving face

Pumpkin in window

Page 104

Empty table

Mat & plate

Utensils added

Drink added

Chicken added

Boy seated

Sequencing • EMC 737